C000101181

MUM

FOR ALL THAT YOU ARE TO ME

summersdale

MUM

Copyright © Summersdale Publishers Ltd, 2018

Compiled by Vicki Vrint

Images © RedKoala/Shutterstock.com

All rights reserved.

No part of this book may be reproduced by any means, nor transmitted, nor translated into a machine language, without the written permission of the publishers.

Condition of Sale
This book is sold subject to the condition that it shall not, by way of trade or otherwise, be lent, resold, hired out or otherwise circulated in any form of binding or cover other than that in which it is published and without a similar condition including this condition being imposed on the subsequent purchaser.

Summersdale Publishers Ltd
46 West Street
Chichester
West Sussex
PO19 1RP
UK

www.summersdale.com

Printed and bound in Croatia

ISBN: 978-1-78685-229-8

Substantial discounts on bulk quantities of Summersdale books are available to corporations, professional associations and other organisations. For details contact general enquiries: telephone: +44 (0) 1243 771107 or email: enquiries@summersdale.com.

TO...

FROM...

A mother is one to
whom you hurry when
you are troubled.

EMILY DICKINSON

Being who you truly
want to be – who you
truly are – is one of the
most important things
my mother taught me.

Kelly Osbourne

YOU'RE
MY
GUIDING
LIGHT.

The moment a child
is born, the mother
is also born.

Bhagwan Shree Rajneesh

THERE ARE
TWO THINGS
WE CAN HOPE
TO GIVE OUR
CHILDREN:
ROOTS AND
WINGS.

We all come from
women, and there's
something extraordinary
about the mothers
who raised us.

Annie Lennox

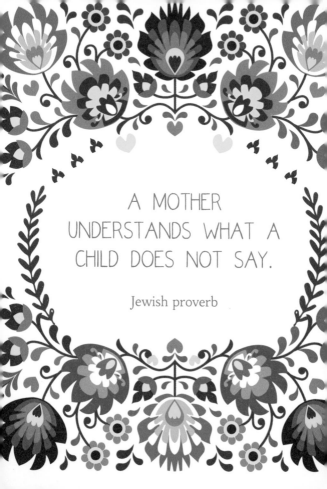

A MOTHER UNDERSTANDS WHAT A CHILD DOES NOT SAY.

Jewish proverb

A MOTHER
CAN DO
MORE IN TEN
MINUTES THAN
MOST PEOPLE
DO IN A DAY.

I BELIEVE THE CHOICE
TO BECOME A MOTHER
IS THE CHOICE TO
BECOME ONE OF THE
GREATEST SPIRITUAL
TEACHERS THERE IS.

Oprah Winfrey

Acceptance, tolerance,
bravery, compassion.
These are the things
my mom taught me.

Lady Gaga

BEING A MOTHER MEANS
THAT YOUR HEART IS
NO LONGER YOURS; IT
WANDERS WHEREVER
YOUR CHILDREN DO.

George Bernard Shaw

A MOTHER'S
HUG LASTS
A LONG TIME
AFTER SHE
LETS
GO.

Being a mother is
exhausting, but it really is
the best job in the world.

SANDRA BULLOCK

A
MOTHER'S
ARMS
ARE THE
SAFEST
PLACE
TO BE.

The joys of parents
are secret; and so are
their griefs and fears.

Francis Bacon

EVERY HOME IS A
UNIVERSITY AND
THE PARENTS ARE
THE TEACHERS.

Mahatma Gandhi

NOTHING
IS LOST
UNTIL YOUR
MOTHER
CAN'T
FIND IT.

IT IS NOT A SLIGHT
THING WHEN THEY,
WHO ARE SO FRESH
FROM GOD, LOVE US.

Charles Dickens

When you look into your mother's eyes, you know that is the purest love you can find on this earth.

Mitch Albom

YOU ALWAYS
KNOW THE
RIGHT THING
TO SAY.

No language can express
the power, and beauty,
and heroism, and majesty
of a mother's love.

Edwin Hubbell Chapin

I MAY BE A NOVICE
BUT I'M LEARNING
FROM THE BEST.

Alex Jones describing her
mother as a role model

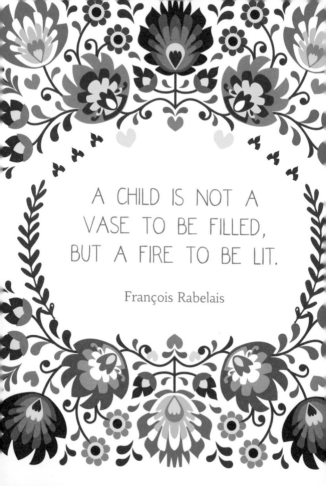

A CHILD IS NOT A
VASE TO BE FILLED,
BUT A FIRE TO BE LIT.

François Rabelais

A friend can't take the
place of a mother;
I need my mother to
set a good example.

ANNE FRANK

WHEREVER
I GO, YOUR
LOVE LIGHTS
MY PATH.

I am sure that if the mothers of various nations could meet, there would be no more wars.

E. M. Forster

YOU'VE GIVEN ME
THE CONFIDENCE
TO BE MYSELF.

THE BIGGEST
LESSON WE
HAVE TO GIVE
OUR CHILDREN
IS TRUTH.

Goldie Hawn

The happiness
of the domestic
fireside is the first
boon of Heaven.

Thomas Jefferson

One good mother
is worth a
hundred teachers.

Italian proverb

YOU'RE THE
KIND OF
PARENT I
HOPE TO BE
ONE DAY.

NO GIFT TO YOUR
MOTHER CAN EQUAL HER
GIFT TO YOU — LIFE.

Anonymous

YOU GO FROM THINKING
OF YOURSELF AS
PRIMARILY AN INDIVIDUAL,
TO SUDDENLY BEING
A MOTHER, FIRST
AND FOREMOST.

Catherine, Duchess of Cambridge

A mother
is a mother
still; the holiest
thing alive.

Samuel Taylor Coleridge

A heart set on love
will do no wrong.

CONFUCIUS

I ADMIT IT — YOU WERE RIGHT ALL ALONG!

Sometimes the strength
of motherhood
is stronger than
natural laws.

Barbara Kingsolver

MOTHER IS THE NAME
FOR GOD IN THE
LIPS AND HEARTS OF
LITTLE CHILDREN.

William Makepeace Thackeray

TO THE WORLD
YOU'RE A
MOTHER, BUT
TO ME YOU'RE
THE WORLD.

You can't give a child
too much love.

John Lennon

YOU TAUGHT ME TO REACH FOR THE STARS.

My mother... shone for
me like the evening star.

WINSTON CHURCHILL

MOTHERS HEAL
EVERYTHING
FROM A
GRAZED KNEE
TO A BROKEN
HEART.

What do girls do who
haven't any mothers
to help them through
their troubles?

Louisa May Alcott

IF EVOLUTION
REALLY WORKS HOW
COME MOTHERS ONLY
HAVE TWO HANDS?

Milton Berle

BECAUSE I'M A MOTHER,
I AM CAPABLE OF
BEING SHOCKED; AS
I NEVER WAS WHEN
I WAS NOT ONE.

Margaret Atwood

MOTHERHOOD HAS
A VERY HUMANISING
EFFECT. EVERYTHING GETS
REDUCED TO ESSENTIALS.

Meryl Streep

In times of test,
family is best.

Burmese proverb

Children have never
been very good at
listening to their elders,
but they have never
failed to imitate them.

James Baldwin

My mother
was the making
of me.

Thomas Edison

[MY MUM] INSTILLED IN ME... THAT WHAT I WAS THINKING AND DOING AND SAYING WERE INFINITELY MORE IMPORTANT THAN MY PHYSICAL APPEARANCE.

Emma Watson

It is not until you become a mother that your judgement slowly turns to compassion and understanding.

Erma Bombeck

YOU CAN FOOL
SOME PEOPLE,
BUT YOU
CAN'T FOOL
YOUR MUM.

A mother is she who
can take the place of all
others but whose place
no one else can take.

CARDINAL MERMILLOD

I feel in contact
with my mother when
I look at my children.
I can feel her influence
over me then.

Angelina Jolie

A MOTHER'S ARMS ARE
MADE OF TENDERNESS
AND CHILDREN SLEEP
SOUNDLY IN THEM.

Victor Hugo

MOTHER:
(NOUN)
TEACHER,
NURSE, GUIDE,
ADVISER,
PROTECTOR,
BEST FRIEND.

YOU LEAN INTO YOUR FAMILY, ASK FOR HELP, AND SHOW COMPASSION.

Liv Tyler

YOU'RE
THE BEST
LISTENER.

My mother is my
root, my foundation.
She planted the seed
that I base my life on.

Michael Jordan

I can't help but be
a different person
now that I've had kids.
That really does change
your whole perspective
on life for the better.

Jennifer Lopez

YOU
ALWAYS
KNOW HOW
TO CHEER
ME UP.

THEY SAY OUR MOTHERS
REALLY KNOW HOW
TO PUSH OUR BUTTONS
— BECAUSE THEY
INSTALLED THEM.

Robin Williams

Let France have good
mothers, and she will
have good sons.

NAPOLEON BONAPARTE

THAT BEST ACADEMY,
A MOTHER'S KNEE.

James Russell Lowell

EVERY BEETLE IS A
GAZELLE IN THE EYES
OF ITS MOTHER.

Moroccan proverb

The very fact that you worry about being a good mom means that you already are one.

Jodi Picoult

Sweater, n: garment
worn by child when its
mother is feeling chilly.

Ambrose Bierce

YOU PICK ME
UP WHEN
LIFE KNOCKS
ME DOWN.

One of the oldest human
needs is having someone
to wonder where you
are when you don't
come home at night.

Margaret Mead

CHILDREN AND MOTHERS
NEVER TRULY PART
— BOUND IN THE
BEATING OF EACH
OTHER'S HEARTS.

Charlotte Gray

YOU'RE
ALWAYS
ON MY
SIDE.

Mom: the person
most likely to write
an autobiography and
never mention herself.

ROBERT BRAULT

THE STRENGTH OF
A NATION DERIVES
FROM THE INTEGRITY
OF THE HOME.

Confucius

Motherhood: all love
begins and ends there.

Robert Browning

I WANT MY CHILDREN TO
HAVE ALL THE THINGS
I COULDN'T AFFORD.
THEN I WANT TO
MOVE IN WITH THEM.

Phyllis Diller

YOU LET ME
MAKE MY OWN
MISTAKES AND
TAUGHT ME
HOW TO PUT
THEM RIGHT.

The heart of a mother
is a deep abyss at the
bottom of which you will
always find forgiveness.

Honoré de Balzac

When children are
doing nothing, they
are doing mischief.

Henry Fielding

THE GREATEST WORK
THAT KINDNESS DOES TO
OTHERS IS THAT IT MAKES
THEM KIND THEMSELVES.

Amelia Earhart

Govern a family as you
would cook a small
fish – very gently.

CHINESE PROVERB

YOU HELD MY
HAND AS A
CHILD, BUT
YOU'LL HOLD
MY HEART
FOREVER.

There's no doubt that motherhood is the best thing in my life. It's all that really matters.

Courtney Cox

YOUR HEART IS
BEATING OUTSIDE
YOUR BODY WHEN
YOU HAVE A BABY.

Kate Beckinsale

I sustain myself with
the love of family.

Maya Angelou

Motherhood meant
I have written four
fewer books, but I
know more about life.

A. S. Byatt

THERE IS NO WAY TO
BE A PERFECT MOTHER,
BUT A MILLION WAYS
TO BE A GOOD ONE.

Jill Churchill

Family faces are magic mirrors – looking at people who belong to us, we see the past, present and future.

Gail Lumet Buckley

I want to give a kid all
of the magical gifts my
mom gave to me, such
as love and friendship.

Jennifer Love Hewitt

I O U
1,000 NIGHTS
OF LOST
SLEEP AND
1,000 CUPS
OF TEA!

Mother's love is peace.
It need not be acquired,
it need not be deserved.

Erich Fromm

CHILDREN REINVENT
YOUR WORLD FOR YOU.

Susan Sarandon

Any kid will
run any errand
for you, if you ask
at bedtime.

Red Skelton

YOU
ALWAYS
KNOW
HOW TO
MAKE
THINGS
BETTER.

SOME ARE KISSING
MOTHERS AND SOME ARE
SCOLDING MOTHERS, BUT IT
IS LOVE JUST THE SAME.

Pearl S. Buck

There is only one pretty child in the world, and every mother has it.

Chinese proverb

YOU'LL
ALWAYS
BE MY
HERO.

THE VISIONS WE
OFFER OUR CHILDREN
SHAPE THE FUTURE.

Carl Sagan

MOTHER: (VERB)
TO LOVE,
PROTECT,
CHERISH AND
CARE FOR.

A mother is the truest
friend we have.

WASHINGTON IRVING

The toughest part of
motherhood is the
inner worrying and
not showing it.

Audrey Hepburn

CHILDREN ARE THE
ANCHORS THAT HOLD
A MOTHER TO LIFE.

Sophocles

LIFE
DOESN'T
COME
WITH A
MANUAL;
IT COMES
WITH A
MOTHER.

You don't choose
your family. They are
God's gift to you, as
you are to them.

Desmond Tutu

IT'S FUNNY HOW A PARENT'S RAISED EYEBROW CAN DO MORE DAMAGE TO YOUR PSYCHE THAN, SAY, CHINESE WATER TORTURE.

Arabella Weir

MOTHER REALLY DOES KNOW BEST.

YOU LOOKED
AFTER ME...
AND TAUGHT
ME HOW TO
LOOK AFTER
MYSELF!

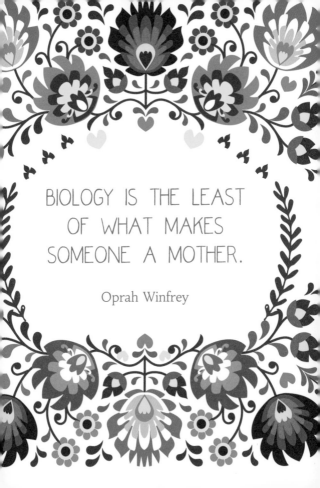

BIOLOGY IS THE LEAST
OF WHAT MAKES
SOMEONE A MOTHER.

Oprah Winfrey

Being a mom has
made me so tired.
And so happy.

TINA FEY

YOU CAN KISS YOUR
FAMILY AND FRIENDS
GOODBYE AND PUT
MILES BETWEEN YOU,
BUT AT THE SAME TIME
YOU CARRY THEM WITH
YOU IN YOUR HEART.

Frederick Buechner

The mother is the most
precious possession
of the nation.

Ellen Key

A mother always
has to think twice,
once for herself and
once for her child.

Sophia Loren

Any mother could
perform the jobs
of several air-traffic
controllers with ease.

Lisa Alther

THERE WAS NEVER A
CHILD SO LOVELY BUT
HIS MOTHER WAS GLAD
TO GET HIM TO SLEEP.

Ralph Waldo Emerson

My mother made me
what I am. She gave
me the greatest gift
a mother can give –
the desire to excel.

Barbara Taylor Bradford

THE FAMILY IS
ONE OF NATURE'S
MASTERPIECES.

George Santayana

MOTHERS GO ON GETTING
BLAMED UNTIL THEY'RE
EIGHTY, BUT SHOULDN'T
TAKE IT PERSONALLY.

Katharine Whitehorn

To describe my mother
would be to write
about a hurricane in
its perfect power.

MAYA ANGELOU

I'D CHOOSE BEING A
MUM OVER MY FOUR
OLYMPIC MEDALS ANY
DAY OF THE WEEK.

Rebecca Adlington

YOU
INSPIRE
ME
EVERY
DAY.

To a child's ear,
'mother' is magic
in any language.

Arlene Benedict

Being a mother has
made my life complete.

Darcey Bussell

YOU ALWAYS
HAVE A SMILE
FOR ME.

My mother had a great
deal of trouble with me,
but I think she enjoyed it.

Mark Twain

MORE THAN ANY OTHER
HUMAN RELATIONSHIP...
MOTHERHOOD MEANS
BEING INSTANTLY
INTERRUPTIBLE,
RESPONSIVE,
RESPONSIBLE.

Tillie Olsen

A mother's arms are
more comforting
than anyone else's.

Diana, Princess of Wales

Family is everything
to me... My family
will always be my
greatest love.

Dolly Parton

NO MATTER HOW OLD
A MOTHER IS, SHE
WATCHES HER MIDDLE-
AGED CHILDREN FOR
SIGNS OF IMPROVEMENT.

Florida Scott-Maxwell

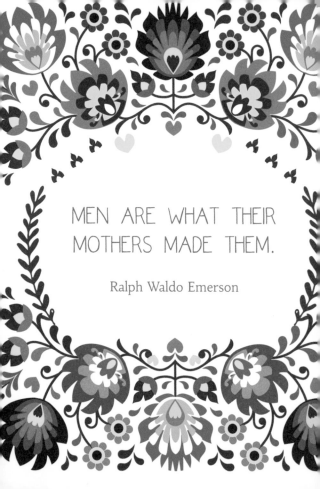

MEN ARE WHAT THEIR
MOTHERS MADE THEM.

Ralph Waldo Emerson

YOU
LOVE ME
NO MATTER
WHAT.

YOU
BRIGHTEN
EVERY
DAY.

THOUGH MOTHERHOOD
IS THE MOST IMPORTANT
OF ALL THE PROFESSIONS...
THERE WAS NO ATTENTION
GIVEN TO PREPARATION
FOR THIS OFFICE.

Elizabeth Cady Stanton

As the family goes, so goes the nation and so goes the whole world in which we live.

POPE JOHN PAUL II

There was never a
great man who had
not a great mother.

Olive Schreiner

YOU
GIVE THE
WARMEST
HUGS.

A MOTHER IS NOT A
PERSON TO LEAN ON,
BUT A PERSON TO MAKE
LEANING UNNECESSARY.

Dorothy Canfield Fisher

YOU'VE
GIVEN ME A
CHILDHOOD
TO CHERISH.

FAMILY IS NOT AN
IMPORTANT THING.
IT'S EVERYTHING.

Michael J. Fox

What I care about
most for children is
that they have passion
and compassion.

Phyllis Logan

BECOMING A MOTHER
MAKES YOU THE MOTHER
OF ALL CHILDREN. FROM
NOW ON EACH WOUNDED,
ABANDONED, FRIGHTENED
CHILD IS YOURS.

Charlotte Gray

YOU'RE
ALWAYS
THERE
FOR
ME.

MOTHER LOVE IS THE
FUEL THAT ENABLES A
NORMAL HUMAN BEING
TO DO THE IMPOSSIBLE.

Marion Garretty

ALL THAT I AM, OR
HOPE TO BE, I OWE TO
MY ANGEL MOTHER.

Abraham Lincoln

YOU'RE IN
ALL MY
HAPPIEST
MEMORIES.

Being a mom is the
most rewarding
feeling in the world.

Kim Kardashian

THE FAMILY. WE WERE
A STRANGE LITTLE
BAND OF CHARACTERS
TRUDGING THROUGH
LIFE SHARING DISEASES
AND TOOTHPASTE,
COVETING ONE
ANOTHER'S DESSERTS.

Erma Bombeck

The art of dealing
with children might
be defined as knowing
what not to say.

A. S. Neill

YOU'RE
ONE
IN A
MILLION.

WHEN YOU LOOK
AT YOUR LIFE, THE
GREATEST HAPPINESSES
ARE FAMILY HAPPINESSES.

Joyce Brothers

THE FIRST CHILD IS
MADE OF GLASS, THE
SECOND OF PORCELAIN,
THE REST OF RUBBER,
STEEL AND GRANITE.

Richard Needham

IT SORT OF PUTS THINGS
INTO PERSPECTIVE, AND
IT'S ABOUT REAL LIFE,
AND LIFE IS ABOUT
PEOPLE, WHAT WE
GIVE, WHAT WE TAKE,
WHAT WE SHARE.

Halle Berry on motherhood

HOME IS
WHERE
YOUR
MUM IS.

WOMEN AS GUARDIANS
OF CHILDREN POSSESS
GREAT POWER. THEY ARE
THE MOULDERS OF THEIR
CHILDREN'S PERSONALITIES
AND THE ARBITERS OF
THEIR DEVELOPMENT.

Ann Oakley

Everything is dear
to its parent.

Sophocles

Mama was my greatest
teacher, a teacher
of compassion, love
and fearlessness.

Stevie Wonder

YOU KNOW
YOU SAID 'ONE
DAY YOU'LL
THANK ME'...
THANK YOU!

If you're interested in finding out more about our books, find us on Facebook at **Summersdale Publishers** and follow us on Twitter at **@Summersdale**.

www.summersdale.com